W9-BHK-888

from SEA TO SHINING SEA

Puerto Rico

By Dennis Brindell Fradin and Judith Bloom Fradin

CONSULTANTS

Carmen Arroyo, M.L.S., Librarian, Center for Advanced Studies on Puerto Rico
and the Caribbean

Robert L. Hillerich, Ph.D., Professor Emeritus, Bowling Green State University;
Consultant, Pinellas County Schools, Florida

CHILDRENS PRESS®
CHICAGO

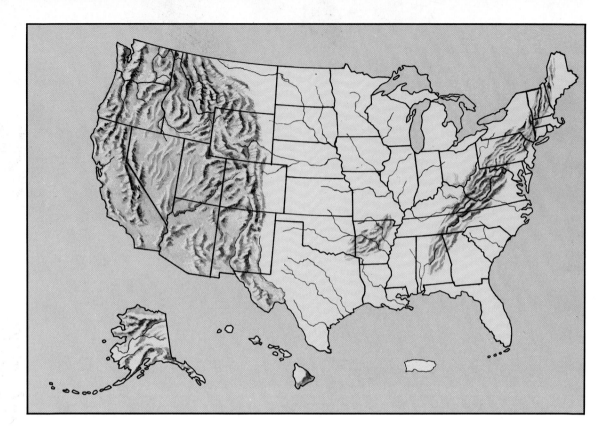

The island of Puerto Rico is a United States commonwealth.

For Fran Dyra, Joan Downing, Mary Reidy, and Margrit Fiddle—the heart of Childrens Press and the best staff an author could work with

For his gracious help, the authors thank Dr. Ricardo Alegría, Director of the Center for Advanced Studies on Puerto Rico and the Caribbean, Old San Juan

Front cover picture: San Juan Gate, fortified wall, and sentry box, Old San Juan; page 1: Grand Regatta; back cover: Cabo Rojo Cliff at Jagüey Point

Project Editor: Joan Downing
Design Director: Karen Kohn
Photo Researcher: Jan Izzo
Typesetting: Graphic Connections, Inc.
Engraving: Liberty Photoengraving

Library of Congress Cataloging-in-Publication Data

Fradin, Dennis B.
  Puerto Rico / by Dennis Brindell Fradin & Judith Bloom Fradin.
    p.   cm. — (From sea to shining sea)
  Includes index.
  Summary: Presents a history and description of this popular vacationland located 1,050 miles southeast of Miami, Florida.
  ISBN 0-516-03856-7
  1. Puerto Rico—Juvenile literature. [1. Puerto Rico.]
I. Fradin, Judith Bloom. II. Title. III. Series: Fradin, Dennis B. From sea to shining sea.
F1958.3.F73   1995   95-16892
972.95—dc20   CIP
                                                               AC

Table of Contents

Costumes worn at the Santiago Apostal Festival, Loiza

Introducing Puerto Rico

Puerto Rico lies 1,000 miles southeast of Florida. This island's name is Spanish, meaning "rich port." Christopher Columbus claimed Puerto Rico for Spain in 1493. The island remained a Spanish colony until 1898. Then the United States gained Puerto Rico from Spain.

Although not a state, the island is part of the United States. In 1952, Puerto Rico became a Commonwealth of the United States. Today, Puerto Rico shows a mix of Spanish and American backgrounds. Puerto Ricans are United States citizens. Yet Spanish is the official language.

Puerto Rico grows large amounts of sugar cane and coffee. Its industries make medicines, sugar, and clothing. Warm weather and sandy beaches bring millions of visitors each year.

*A picture map
of Puerto Rico*

Puerto Rico is special in other ways. Where is the United States Forest Service's only tropical rain forest? Where is the giant Arecibo Observatory radio telescope? Where are loud tree frogs called *coquís* found? Where were baseball legend Roberto Clemente and actress Rita Moreno born? The answer to these questions is: Puerto Rico!

Overleaf: The El Yunque Rain Forest

5

Island of Mountains, Valleys, and Beaches

ISLAND OF MOUNTAINS, VALLEYS, AND BEACHES

The Virgin Islands and Hispaniola are also islands in the West Indies. Hispaniola contains the countries of Haiti and the Dominican Republic.

Plantains border Guajataca Lake

Puerto Rico is an island. It's part of the West Indies. The Atlantic Ocean splashes to the north. The Caribbean Sea rolls to the south. The island of Hispaniola lies to the west. The Virgin Islands are to the east.

Smaller islands are also part of Puerto Rico. Vieques and Culebra islands are to the east. Mona Island is to the west. Altogether, Puerto Rico covers 3,515 square miles. Among the fifty states, only Rhode Island and Delaware are smaller.

Three-fourths of Puerto Rico has hills or mountains. Coffee is grown in the mountain valleys. Cerro de Punta is the island's highest peak. It stands near the island's center. Cerro de Punta rises 4,389 feet above sea level.

The island also has a 311-mile seacoast. Lowlands line Puerto Rico's northern and southern coasts. Beautiful valleys edge the western and eastern coasts. Sugar cane and coconuts are grown along the coasts. Puerto Rico's largest cities are found there, too.

Puerto Rico has few natural lakes. The island does have lakes formed by damming rivers. Some of

them are lakes Cidra, Guajataca, and Yauco. About fifty rivers twist through Puerto Rico. All are short and fairly shallow. That's why big ships can't travel on them. Río de la Plata is 46 miles long. It's Puerto Rico's longest river. Other rivers are the Loíza and the Arecibo.

PLANTS AND ANIMALS

Puerto Rico has many different plants and animals. Some are found nowhere else in the United States. One-fifth of the island is wooded. The ceiba tree produces kapok. This is used to fill mattresses and bases for baseball. Mahogany trees are used to make lovely furniture. Poincianas have beautiful red blossoms. Other Puerto Rican trees are flamboyants, tamarinds, and cassias.

The *coquí* is a tree frog. It's just two inches long.

A green sea turtle

Humpback whales have big flippers and reach 50-foot lengths. Manatees are nicknamed sea cows. They weigh up to 3,500 pounds.

An upside-down jellyfish

Its two-note song is "Ko-kee! Ko-kee!" The *paso fino* is a small horse. It's known for its graceful gait. Mongooses kill Puerto Rico's rats and snakes. The commonwealth's biggest snake is the Puerto Rican boa. It can grow to be 7 feet long. The *araña boba* ("silly spider") is a scary-looking spider. It is really harmless. However, Puerto Rico's giant centipedes give a painful bite. They grow to be 15 inches or longer.

Humpback whales and manatees swim along the coasts. Sea turtles often climb onto Puerto Rico's shore. Jellyfish are bell-shaped sea animals. They sting swimmers along the coast. Starfish, seahorses, and sea cucumbers are ocean animals that live among sea corals.

Hundreds of kinds of birds fly about Puerto Rico. The *reinita* ("little queen") loves sweets. It sometimes flies through open windows and grabs sugar from tables. The Puerto Rican parrot lives only in Puerto Rico.

CLIMATE

Puerto Rico is south of the Tropic of Cancer. That's why it has a warm, wet climate. Trade winds blow across Puerto Rico. These ocean breezes help cool

the island. Temperatures above 70 degrees Fahrenheit are typical all year. Snow never falls on Puerto Rico. But rain falls almost every day somewhere in Puerto Rico. The El Yunque Rain Forest receives about 200 inches of rain a year. That's more than half an inch of rain a day! The southern coast gets less than 40 inches of rain a year.

Now and then, hurricanes strike Puerto Rico. These storms build up over the ocean. They have strong winds. In 1928, the San Felipe hurricane hit Puerto Rico. Its 200-mile-per-hour winds killed about 300 people. In 1989, Hurricane Hugo killed twelve people. It caused $1 billion in damages.

Overleaf: The Ponce Market in the 1890s

From Ancient Times Until Today

Over 185 million years ago, Puerto Rico was part of a large landmass. It stretched from Cuba to Mexico and South America. Then the land sank under the Atlantic Ocean. Over time, volcanoes erupted beneath the sea. They formed underwater mountains. Earthquakes pushed the mountains above the sea. Puerto Rico and other West Indies islands were formed in this way.

Puerto Rico's Indians

Archaic Indians reached Puerto Rico about 4,000 years ago. They may have come in log boats from present-day Florida. These people settled along Puerto Rico's coast. They fished. They also gathered clams and oysters.

About 1,900 years ago, Arawak Indians arrived. They rowed canoes from South America. The Arawaks were farmers. They built villages near the coast. Slowly, they conquered the fishing Indians. Over time, other groups of Arawaks arrived from South America. In 1948, Arawak tools and pots were found in a coastal cave.

13

A Taíno Indian village has been reconstructed at the Tibes Indian Ceremonial Center.

By the 1400s, Puerto Rico's Indians called themselves *Taínos*. That means "the good ones." The Taínos name for Puerto Rico was *Borinquén*. That means "land of the brave lord." The Taínos lived in villages throughout Borinquén. They built huts of wood, leaves, and vines. They slept in cotton *hamacas*. These swinging beds are like present-day hammocks. The Taínos grew tobacco, corn, pineapples, manioc, and sweet potatoes. Cotton grew wild. The Taínos also hunted and fished. By the late 1400s, perhaps 40,000 Taínos lived in Puerto Rico.

14

Spanish Conquest and Rule

In 1493, Christopher Columbus made his second trip to the West Indies. On November 19, 1493, he reached present-day Puerto Rico. Columbus was Puerto Rico's first-known European visitor. He claimed the island for Spain. Columbus named the island San Juan Bautista. Soon Columbus sailed for Hispaniola. He had claimed that island for Spain in 1492.

Puerto Rico was the only place in what is now the United States that Columbus ever visited.

In 1508, Juan Ponce de León came to San Juan Bautista. He founded Caparra. That was Puerto Rico's first European settlement. It stood near present-day San Juan. Ponce de León served as Puerto Rico's first Spanish governor.

The Spaniards enslaved the Taínos. They made the Indians mine gold. In 1511, Agüeybaná the Brave led an Indian revolt. But Indian stone axes were no match for Spanish swords and guns. Agüeybaná and many other Indians were killed. Thousands of Indians fled the island by canoe.

Juan Ponce de León

In 1521, Caparra was moved to present-day San Juan. But the Spaniards called the city *Puerto Rico.* That meant "rich port." By the 1530s, the island was running out of gold. Many of the Taíno slaves had died. The Spaniards then began growing sugar

15

cane. To do the work, they brought in African slaves. By 1531, there were about 2,000 African slaves in Puerto Rico. Only 500 Spaniards lived on the island.

Puerto Rico meant more to Spain than gold and sugar. It became known as the "Key to the West Indies." Puerto Rico guarded other Spanish lands to the west and south. Spain built forts on Puerto Rico. Spanish soldiers came to run the forts. Work began on El Morro in 1539. This huge fort still stands in San Juan.

El Morro

In 1595, English sea captain Sir Francis Drake attacked San Juan. Spanish soldiers fired cannons at the English ships. The English suffered great losses. They sailed away in defeat. The English attacked again in 1598. They took San Juan but lost many men. In the streets of San Juan, Puerto Ricans continued to fight. They threw stones at the English soldiers. After two months, the English fled. Before they left, they burned most of San Juan.

In this battle, a cannonball just missed Drake but killed two men in his cabin.

The Dutch attacked San Juan in 1625. Puerto Ricans fought them for weeks. Finally, the Dutch leader wrote to Puerto Rico's governor. He said to surrender San Juan or the Dutch would burn it. Governor Juan de Haro wrote back: "The settlers have enough courage to rebuild their houses. Do as you please!" The Dutch set fire to San Juan. Then they, too, sailed away. Once again, the town was rebuilt. Puerto Ricans became known as proud defenders of their island.

As the years passed, new towns were founded. Ponce was begun in the late 1600s. Mayagüez was founded in 1760. Humacao was founded in 1793. By 1800, Puerto Rico had thirty-nine towns and more than 150,000 people.

Wealthy Spaniards owned large plantations. On them, they grew coffee and tobacco. They also

Luis Muñoz Rivera

raised cattle. The Spaniards still used slaves to do the work. The poor Puerto Rican farmers were called *jíbaros*. They did their own work. Most of them didn't own any land.

By the 1850s, many Puerto Ricans started asking for changes. They wanted more freedom from Spain. Some wanted the slaves freed. They also wanted a better life for Puerto Rico's poor. But Spain ruled the island with an iron fist.

Ramón Emeterio Betances was a doctor. He formed the Puerto Rico Revolutionary Committee. People around the island joined this rebel group. Members used the letters *L* and *M* as their password. These letters stood for *Libertad o Muerte.* That is Spanish meaning "liberty or death." In 1868, Betances led a revolt. The rebels set up the Republic of Puerto Rico. Spanish soldiers hunted down the rebels. Many were killed or jailed.

Later, some changes did take place. On March 22, 1873, slavery was outlawed in Puerto Rico. About 32,000 people gained their freedom. In November 1897, Spain gave Puerto Rico some self-government. Puerto Rican leader Luis Muñoz Rivera helped arrange this. Puerto Rico's government swung into action on July 17, 1898. Earlier that year, Spain and the United States had gone to

war. On July 25, 1898, American soldiers invaded Puerto Rico.

American troops landing at Arroyo in August 1898

UNDER UNITED STATES RULE

The United States won the Spanish-American War in August 1898. Puerto Rico passed to the United States as a prize of war. Now, the United States ran Puerto Rico's government.

The United States also gained the Philippines and Cuba from Spain as a result of the war.

Some Puerto Ricans mourned the loss of self-government. Others welcomed United States rule. They hoped that the United States would help their island. Puerto Rico was very poor. Only a few

Eleanor Roosevelt, wife of President Franklin Delano Roosevelt, on a visit to Puerto Rico

people could read and write. Even fewer people owned land.

Some things did improve. Schools, roads, and hospitals were built. In March 1917, President Woodrow Wilson signed the Jones Act. Through it, Puerto Ricans became United States citizens. They also could have their own senate. In 1917, the United States entered World War I (1914-1918). About 18,000 Puerto Ricans helped the United States win that war.

Yet many Puerto Ricans remained poor. American companies had taken over Puerto Rican sugar, tobacco, and coffee plantations. Thousands of Puerto Ricans worked on these large farms. They received little pay. The Great Depression (1929-1939) made things worse. All over the world, people lost their jobs. Masses of Puerto Ricans went hungry. The island was called the "poorhouse of the Caribbean."

Puerto Rico's hard times started a drive for independence. Some Puerto Ricans called for an uprising against the United States. In 1937, pro-independence people marched in Ponce. The police fired at them. Twenty-one people were killed in the Ponce Massacre. More than 100 were wounded.

In 1938, Luis Muñoz Marín founded a new political party. It was called the *Partido Popular*

Twenty-one people were killed in the Ponce Massacre.

Luis Muñoz Marín was the son of Luis Muñoz Rivera. Many Puerto Ricans follow the Spanish tradition of using the last names of both parents. The father's last name becomes the child's first last name.

Democrático. In English, it is known as the Popular Democratic Party (PDP). The PDP chose a picture of a *jíbaro* as its emblem. This showed that it was a voice for poor people. The PDP is still a major party on the island today.

In 1941, the United States entered World War II (1939-1945). The "Key to the West Indies" helped defend the Caribbean. Puerto Rico sent 65,000 people into service.

THE COMMONWEALTH OF PUERTO RICO

Luis Muñoz Marín (in tie) founded the Popular Democratic Party.

About 2 million people lived in Puerto Rico by 1945. Little by little, they began to receive political power. Since 1898, United States presidents had

appointed Puerto Rico's governors. These men had come from the American mainland. Most of them didn't speak Spanish. That's the island's major language. Few knew about Puerto Rican culture. Then, in 1946, President Harry Truman named Jesús T. Piñero as governor. Piñero was the first Puerto Rican-born governor under United States rule.

In 1947, Congress passed a law that allowed Puerto Ricans to elect their own governor. The people elected Luis Muñoz Marín. In 1950, the United States Congress passed the Constitution Act. It gave Puerto Rico the option of becoming a United States commonwealth. In 1951, Puerto Ricans voted to do this. They then wrote a constitution. Puerto Rico became a commonwealth on July 25, 1952. As such, it gained more independence.

In some ways, Puerto Rico is like a state. Like each state, Puerto Rico has a governor. It also has a senate and a house of representatives. In addition, the island is divided into seventy-eight municipalities. Each of these units has its own officials. In other ways, Puerto Rico is almost like another country. Puerto Ricans don't pay income taxes to the United States and they don't vote to elect the president.

During the 1950s, thousands of Puerto Ricans moved to the United States. Most of them settled in

Jesús T. Piñero taking the oath of office as governor of Puerto Rico

Today, about 3 million Puerto Ricans live in the United States. More than one-third of them are in New York City.

northern cities. However, Puerto Ricans often found only low-paying jobs and poor schools.

Meanwhile, life was improving on the island. Governor Luis Muñoz Marín started "Operation Bootstrap." This program brought new businesses to the island. Section 936 of the United States tax code aided "Operation Bootstrap." It gave tax breaks to companies that settled in Puerto Rico. These companies make goods ranging from chemicals to floppy disks. Tourism has also grown in Puerto Rico. Millions of people visit the island each year.

Many Puerto Ricans saw a chance for a better life on the island. They returned from the states. The island's population was 2.7 million in 1970. By 1990, it topped 3.5 million.

Compared to other Caribbean and South American countries, Puerto Rico is rich. But compared to the fifty states, Puerto Rico is still poor. Its jobless rate is about three times as high as in the states. Puerto Rico also has a high murder rate. Drug addiction and AIDS are other huge problems.

Puerto Ricans disagree about how to solve their problems. A big question is whether or not to remain a commonwealth. Many people favor the commonwealth. Others think Puerto Rico should become a state. A third group wants Puerto Rico to

This high-technology Puerto Rican company makes circuit boards.

become a separate country. This, they claim, would best preserve Puerto Rican culture.

Islanders voted on the issue in 1967 and 1993. In 1967, three-fifths of the voters chose to remain a commonwealth. The 1993 vote was closer. That time, less than one-half wanted to stay a commonwealth. Nearly as many voters chose statehood. But only one of twenty-five voters favored independence. Many people feel that Puerto Rico will soon become America's fifty-first state.

The year 1993 marked 500 years since Columbus's arrival. Puerto Rico has undergone great changes since 1493. No one knows what the next 500 years will bring. But Puerto Ricans will continue to improve life on their island.

Cruise ships at Old San Juan

Overleaf: A young Puerto Rican girl with flowers in her hair

Puerto Ricans and Their Work

PUERTO RICANS AND THEIR WORK

I n 1990, Puerto Rico had more than 3.5 million people. For its size, Puerto Rico is very crowded. About 1,000 people live in each square mile. New Jersey is the only state that is as crowded.

Over 99 of 100 Puerto Ricans have some Hispanic background. Many are also part Indian or African. A few Puerto Ricans have come from Portugal, Italy, and South America. Spanish is the island's main language. Many Puerto Ricans also speak English. Some Puerto Ricans have spent many years in the states. When they return to the island, they speak *Spanglish*. This is a blend of Spanish and English.

About 85 of 100 Puerto Ricans are Catholic. The island has some Protestants and Jews, too. Some Puerto Rican Christians also follow *espiritismo*. This is a mix of Catholic, Indian, and African beliefs.

PUERTO RICANS AT WORK

More than 1 million Puerto Ricans have jobs. Government and service work are the leading fields.

A Christmas parade in Old San Juan

Families at the Maricao Coffee Festival

About 4 million people visit Puerto Rico each year.

Left: A Puerto Rican policewoman
Right: Workers assembling computer circuits

Each has about 220,000 workers. Letter carriers, police, and teachers are among the government workers. Many Puerto Rican service workers have jobs in hotels. They serve Puerto Rico's visitors. Other service workers are doctors, nurses, and lawyers. Still others fix cars or computers. About 200,000 Puerto Ricans sell goods. They work in shops, stores, and restaurants.

About 170,000 people make goods in Puerto Rico. Medicine is the island's top product. Puerto Rico is a world leader at making medicines. Machin-

ery and other metal goods are the second-leading product group. Puerto Ricans also make medical and scientific instruments. Sugar is made in Puerto Rico's sugar mills. It comes from the island's sugar cane. Puerto Rican rum is a well-known alcoholic drink. Clothing is also produced in Puerto Rico.

About 35,000 Puerto Ricans farm or fish. They grow sugar cane, coffee, bananas, coconuts, pineapples, and oranges. Beef cattle, milk, chickens, and eggs are other farm goods. Lobsters are the main fishing product. Other catches include tuna and snapper.

Left: A lobster fisherman
Right: A fruit stand owner peeling oranges

Overleaf: An evening view of La Fortaleza (now the governor's mansion) from the water

29

A Tour of Puerto Rico

A Tour of Puerto Rico

Puerto Rico has sunny beaches and a rain forest. It has old Spanish forts and a big radio telescope. Friendly people and colorful towns add to Puerto Rico's charm.

San Juan

San Juan is on the northeast coast. It's a good place to start a tour of Puerto Rico. San Juan dates from 1521. It is Puerto Rico's capital. It's also the island's biggest city. Old San Juan is filled with the city's history. In the Plaza de Colón stands a statue of Cristóbal Colón. That is the Spanish spelling of Christopher Columbus. Three great forts are also in Old San Juan. La Fortaleza is the oldest. It was begun in 1532. Today, La Fortaleza serves as the home of Puerto Rico's governor. El Morro was begun in 1539. It has 20-foot-thick walls. San Cristóbal is the largest Spanish fort built in the New World. It has hidden tunnels. They were used to move men and supplies during battles.

Casa Blanca is the island's oldest house. It's another landmark of Old San Juan. Casa Blanca was

The statue of Christopher Columbus in Old San Juan

built for Ponce de Leon's family in the 1520s. San Juan Cathedral is one of the New World's oldest churches. The first building was finished in 1530. Ponce de León's remains were buried there in 1908.

San Juan's Museum of Santos has colorful carvings of *santos* (saints). The carvings are an old Puerto Rican art form. According to the Catholic faith, saints are the good who have died and gone to heaven.

New San Juan has the city's more modern places. Restaurants, stores, and offices stand in New San Juan. Hotels line the beaches. El Capitolio is in

La Fortaleza

An interior view of Casa Blanca, Puerto Rico's oldest house

The capitol

New San Juan. This is Puerto Rico's capitol building. Inside it are pictures showing major events in Puerto Rico's past.

NEAR SAN JUAN

Bayamón is to the west of San Juan. Settlers led by Ponce de León began Bayamón in 1509. Bayamón is Puerto Rico's second-largest city. Bayamón's city hall was built in 1978. It rises above a highway. Bayamón also has many new office buildings and apartments. But the city has kept some old ways, too. People still sell bread and roasted chicken along roads entering the city.

The Francisco Oller Art Museum is in Bayamón. Many of this Bayamón artist's 800 paintings hang there. Oller showed how cruel slavery was. He worked to outlaw slavery in Puerto Rico. The restored home of José Celso Barbosa is also in Bayamón. He was a black doctor, educator, and political leader. Barbosa worked for Puerto Rican statehood. Bayamón also has outstanding science museums. They are at the Luis A. Ferré Science Park.

Carolina is just east of San Juan. It's the island's fourth-largest city. The Roberto Clemente Sports City is in Carolina. It offers children sports and art activities. Roberto Clemente was born in Carolina. A mural of Clemente is also in the city. Nearby is the town of Hato Rey. Roberto Clemente Stadium stands there.

To the south of San Juan is Río Piedras. The largest branch of the University of Puerto Rico is there. About 19,000 students go to the college in Río Piedras. It is known for its fine teachers. Juan Ramón Jiménez taught poetry there. In 1956, he won the Nobel Prize for literature. Many visitors enjoy the college's Botanical Garden. Over 200

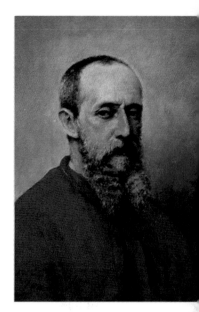

Francisco Oller

The University of Puerto Rico

kinds of tropical plants grow there. The Puerto Rico Symphony Orchestra often plays there.

OTHER HIGHLIGHTS OF EASTERN PUERTO RICO

Luquillo is east of San Juan. Luquillo Beach has white sands, green trees, and blue ocean waters. Many people consider it the island's loveliest beach.

Fajardo is at the island's northeast tip. In the 1700s, it was a supply port for pirates. Cabezas de San Juan Nature Reserve is near Fajardo. Mangrove trees grow there along the ocean. They have

Luquillo Beach

strange-looking roots. The reserve also has cliffs and lagoons. Coral reefs can be seen there, too. They were formed by tiny sea animals. El Faro is another highlight of the reserve. It's a lighthouse built about 1880. From it, visitors can see faraway Caribbean islands.

Boats leave Fajardo each day for Puerto Rico's islands of Culebra and Vieques. Pirate Henry Morgan reportedly buried treasure on Culebra. Today, leatherback turtles nest on Culebra's beaches. They weigh up to 1,200 pounds. That makes leatherbacks the world's largest turtles. The island is also a good place to view water birds. Laughing gulls, pelicans, and boobies can be seen there. The boobies' name comes from *bobo.* That's Spanish meaning "stupid." Sailors coined the name because they caught the birds so easily.

Vieques Island is known for its wild *paso fino* horses. Phosphorescent Bay is on the Island's south coast. Its waters have a strange greenish glow at night. Zillions of tiny water creatures cause this wonder.

Back on the main island is the Caribbean National Forest: El Yunque Rain Forest. This forest is just a few miles inland from the northeast coast. Rain falls there about five times a day. Altogether, El

Blue footed boobies

El Yunque Rain Forest (above) is the United States Forest Service's only tropical rain forest.

Yunque gets about 240 inches of rain a year. That's 100 billion gallons of water. About 250 kinds of trees grow in this rain forest. No other United States national forest has that many. About thirty of these trees grow nowhere else. The rain forest has plants with huge leaves. Some look like elephant ears. Many strong vines also grow in El Yunque. A person could swing on them for miles without touching the ground. Waterfalls tumble through the forest. Coquís chirp as night falls.

To the southeast is Caguas. This city was named for a Taíno who was a leader about 600 years ago. Today, Caguas is Puerto Rico's fifth-largest city. Puerto Rico's cities and towns are known for their plazas. These are public squares. Plaza Palmer is the center of Caguas's life. Musicians play salsa from its bandstand. A huge clock face made of planted flowers is there, too.

Humacao is to the southeast. It lies about midway along Puerto Rico's east coast. Heart pacemakers are made there. It's also great sugar cane country. Just off the coast is Cayo Santiago. Monkeys were brought from India to this little island in 1938. Scientists studied them. During World War II, the monkeys almost starved to death. People from Humacao brought bananas and coconuts for them to eat. Today, nearly 1,000 monkeys live on Cayo Santiago.

Guayama lies along the southeast coast. Early each year, this city hosts the Paso Fino Horse Show. Museo Cautino is an old mansion in town. Visitors can learn what life was like in the late 1800s. Pictures of prize-winning *paso fino* horses can also be seen.

Paso Fino competition

WESTERN PUERTO RICO

Ponce is on the southern coast. Today, Ponce is Puerto Rico's third-largest city. The city is Puerto

Ponce (below) is nicknamed La Perla del Sur—*"The Pearl of the South."*

The Parque de Bombas (firehouse) in Ponce

Rico's major port on the Caribbean. Ponce is also known for its beautiful plazas, parks, and public buildings.

Ponce has one of the Caribbean's best art museums—the Ponce Art Museum. Great European and Puerto Rican works can be seen there. *The Sleep of King Arthur in Avalon* is a favorite work. Ponce also has a flame-red firehouse. It was built in 1883. Today, it's a museum that tells the history of Ponce. Each February, Ponce holds the Festival of Our Lady of Guadalupe. People parade around in strange masks. The tradition goes back over 500 years to Spain.

North of Ponce is the Tibes Indian Ceremonial Center. A 1976 rainstorm helped uncover an ancient Indian center there. Human skeletons dating back about 1,700 years were found. So were ball courts and ceremonial dance grounds. A Taíno village has been rebuilt at Tibes.

Southwest Puerto Rico also has a Phosphorescent Bay. Boats take people out on the bay. On moonless nights, the water glows in the dark. This happens when tiny sea animals move about.

Mona Island is about 40 miles west of Phosphorescent Bay. The island is ringed by 200-foot-high cliffs. Cactus plants grow on Mona Island. Iguanas live there, too. They are Puerto Rico's largest lizards. Long ago, Taíno Indians once lived there. Today, no one lives on the islands. Visitors get there by boat or plane. They can hike around for a few hours.

Mayagüez is midway along Puerto Rico's west coast. This city is a fish-packing center. More than half the tuna eaten in the United States is packed there. Many companies that make medicines have moved there. South of town is an old pirates' hangout. Today, Puerto Ricans vacation on its white-

Masked dancers at the Festival of Our Lady of Guadalupe in Ponce

41

sand beaches. North of town is the Mayagüez Zoo. Animals live there much as they do in the wild. Lions, tigers, and lemurs are among the zoo's animals.

Aguadilla and Aguada are near Puerto Rico's northwest tip. These seaside towns have a friendly rivalry. Both claim to be Columbus's first landing place. Both towns have many *paradors*. These are country inns. *Paradors* are found throughout Puerto Rico. Many are in old coffee plantation houses. Aguadilla is known for its craftspeople. They make wicker hats and lace. Of the two towns, Aguada has the best beaches.

Arecibo is on the north coast. It's about 50 miles west of San Juan. Arecibo is one of Puerto Rico's oldest towns. It dates back to 1556. Today, Arecibo is Puerto Rico's center for making medicines.

South of the city is the Arecibo Observatory. This has the world's largest radio telescope. The giant dish is 1,000 feet across. It's in a large crater in the earth. Visitors can see the radio telescope from a viewing platform. In 1992, this telescope found the first planets beyond earth's solar system. Is anyone on a faraway planet sending signals to earth? The Arecibo telescope has been used to try to

The Arecibo Observatory

answer this question. The project is called the Search for Extra-Terrestrial Intelligence.

Río Camuy Cave Park is north of Arecibo. It's a good place to end a tour of Puerto Rico. Río Camuy has one of the world's largest networks of caves. Within them is the world's second-largest underground river. A big waterfall is also in the cave. The air outside the cave is warmer than the air inside. That's why Río Camuy seems to "breathe" out a kind of fog. The park also has sinkholes. These are large holes in the ground. Water formed them over long periods of time.

Farmland near Arecibo

Overleaf: Roberto Clemente

43

A Gallery of Famous
Puerto Ricans

A GALLERY OF FAMOUS PUERTO RICANS

*P*uerto Rico has produced many famous people. They range from government leaders to baseball stars. Others have become great teachers, musicians, and actors.

Luis Muñoz Rivera (1859-1916) was born in Barranquitas. He was a poet, journalist, and statesman. Muñoz Rivera helped win self-government for Puerto Rico in 1897. He then headed Puerto Rico's new government in 1898. **Luis Muñoz Marín** (1898-1980) was born in San Juan. He was Muñoz Rivera's son. He, too, was a writer and government leader. Muñoz Marín served as Puerto Rico's first elected governor (1949-1965). He set up Operation Bootstrap. It fought poverty in Puerto Rico.

Felisa Rincón de Gautier (1897-1994) was born in Ceiba. In 1932, she helped Puerto Rican women win the vote. Later, Rincón de Gautier served as San Juan's mayor (1946-1968). As mayor of San Juan, she improved roads, housing, and schools.

Ana Méndez was born in Aguada in 1908. She became a high school history teacher. Méndez wanted her students to continue their education. In

Luis Muñoz Rivera Day is celebrated in Puerto Rico on July 17—his birthday.

Mayor Rincón de Gautier

45

1949, she began a college in a garage. It grew into the Ana Méndez University System. Today, it serves 17,000 students.

Lola Rodríguez de Tío (1843?-1924) was born in San Germán. Rodríguez de Tío spoke out for Puerto Rican independence. Forced to leave Puerto Rico, she went to Cuba. There, she wrote the well-known lines: "Cuba and Puerto Rico are one bird with two wings. They receive bullets and flowers through the same heart." Rodríguez de Tío was called "Daughter of the Islands." She wrote the original words to "La Borinqueña," Puerto Rico's anthem. However, her words are no longer used for the song.

Luis Rafael Sánchez was born in Humacao in 1936. He became an author. *Macho Camacho's Beat* is one of his novels. It's about present-day Puerto Rico. His book *The Air Bus* was made into a movie in 1994. It describes Puerto Rican culture through poems, stories, and interviews.

Puerto Rico has produced some fine actors. **José Ferrer** (1912-1992) was born in Santurce. He was known for his deep voice. In 1950, Ferrer won an Academy Award for *Cyrano de Bergerac.* **Raul Julia** (1940-1994) was born in San Juan. He played the devil in a first-grade play. Later, Julia was Rafael

José Ferrer as
Cyrano de Bergerac

on "Sesame Street." His many films include *The Addams Family*. **Rita Moreno** was born in Humacao in 1931. She became a great actress, singer, and dancer. She won an Academy Award for playing Anita in the movie musical *West Side Story*. She won Emmy Awards for "The Muppet Show" and "Rockford Files."

Pablo Casals (1876-1973) was born in Spain. He became a great cellist. In 1956, he moved to Puerto Rico. Casals taught at the University of Puerto Rico in Río Piedras. A music festival in San Juan was named for him. The Casals Festival attracts musicians from around the world. **Justino Díaz** was

Left: Rita Moreno and George Chakiris won Oscars for their roles in West Side Story. *Right: Pablo Casals*

47

José Feliciano

Antonia Novello

born in San Juan in 1940. Díaz became an opera star. **José Feliciano** was born in Lares in 1945. This Puerto Rican musician has been blind all his life. As a child, he listened to singers on the radio. "That's what I want to be," he told people. Feliciano became a singer and guitarist. He has won six Grammy awards.

Myrna Baez was born in San Juan in 1931. She studied in Puerto Rico, Spain, and New York. Her paintings and engravings have won many awards. *El juez* (The Judge) is one of her famous works.

Antonia Coello Novello was born in Fajardo in 1944. She was a sickly child. Novello spent many months in Puerto Rican hospitals. She dreamed of becoming a children's doctor. Novello became a pediatrician. In 1990, she was named Surgeon General of the United States. Dr. Novello worked to improve women's and children's health.

Sixto Escobar (1913-1979) and **Carlos Juan Ortiz** (born 1936) are famous names in boxing. Escobar was born in Barceloneta. His fighting weight was just 118 pounds. Escobar was world bantam-weight champion during the 1930s. Ortiz was born in Ponce. He was the lightweight champ of the 1960s.

Juan "Chi Chi" Rodríguez was born near San Juan in 1935. At six, he became a golf caddy. Chi

Left: Sixto Escobar
Right: "Chi Chi" Rodriguez

Chi wanted to play golf. He didn't have enough money to buy clubs. So Chi Chi made a club out of a tree branch. He learned to play by hitting tin cans. Rodríguez has won many tournaments. Fans love the way he dances around on the course.

Angel Cordero was born in Santurce in 1942. His father and grandfather were jockeys. Cordero could ride a pony at age three. He, too, became a great jockey. Cordero has ridden three Kentucky Derby winners.

Baseball is Puerto Rico's national sport. The island has produced many major-league players.

Angel Cordero

Hiram Bithorn (1916-1952) was born in Santurce. He pitched for the Chicago Cubs in the 1940s. In 1943, he led the league with seven shutouts. San Juan's Bithorn Stadium was named for him.

Hiram Bithorn

Roberto Clemente (1934-1972) was born in Carolina. By age fourteen, he was playing practice games against big leaguers. Clemente's lifetime average was .317. He won four batting crowns. He led the Pittsburgh Pirates to two World Series wins. Clemente's throwing arm was probably the strongest of any outfielder ever. He could throw a baseball more than 400 feet to home plate. Clemente also helped people in many ways. In 1972, he was bringing supplies to earthquake victims in Nicaragua. He died when the plane crashed while taking off from Puerto Rico.

Orlando Cepeda was born in Ponce in 1937. He played seventeen years in the big leagues. Cepeda hit .300 in nine seasons. He hit twenty-five or more home runs for eight seasons. Cepeda won the 1967 Most Valuable Player award.

The Alomars are a Puerto Rican baseball family. **Sandy Alomar, Sr.,** was born in Salinas in 1943. He stole twenty or more bases in seven big-league seasons. **Sandy Alomar, Jr.,** was born in Salinas in 1966. **Roberto Alomar** was born in Ponce in 1968. They are his sons. Sandy, Jr., is a catcher. He was the 1990 American League Rookie of the Year. Roberto is a second baseman. He helped the Toronto Blue Jays win two World Series (1992, 1993).

Juan "Igor" González was born in Vega Baja in 1969. He won the 1992 American League home-run crown. González hit forty-three homers that season. In 1993, he blasted forty-six homers, winning the title again.

Beatriz "Gigi" Fernández was born in San Juan in 1964. Her parents bought her a tennis racket for her eighth birthday. Fernández grew up to be one of tennis's top doubles players. She and her partner won gold medals at the 1992 Olympics. In

1994, she and her partners won the French, British, and Australian championships.

The birthplace of Roberto Clemente, Antonia Coello Novello, and Luis Muñoz Marín . . .

Home, too, of Felisa Rincón de Gautier, Angel Cordero, and Pablo Casals . . .

The site of Arecibo Observatory, El Yunque Rain Forest, and two phosphorescent bays . . .

Today, a popular vacation spot . . .

This is the beautiful island commonwealth—Puerto Rico!

Roberto Alomar is on the left in this picture and his brother, Sandy Alomar, Jr., is on the right. Their father, Sandy Alomar, Sr., played every position in the big leagues but pitcher and catcher.

Did You Know?

The Guánica Dry Forest is west of Ponce. Cactus plants and 250 kinds of trees grow there. Nearly 100 types of birds are also found in the dry forest.

Adjuntas has the United States' lowest ZIP Code—00601.

According to legend, a monster lizard lives in the forests of the island of Culebra.

Recently, San Juan has become the world's number-one port for cruise ships. In the early 1990s, more than 1 million people a year visited Puerto Rico from them.

According to legend, coquís are descended from a beautiful bird that lost its wings. Another old belief is that anyone who sees one of the little frogs while it is singing will enjoy good fortune. But coquís are more often heard than seen. Their musical call has been called Puerto Rico's unofficial national anthem. The coquí is so popular in Puerto Rico that it appears on billboards and T-shirts.

The Atlantic Ocean's deepest known point is north of Puerto Rico. The Puerto Rico Trench goes down 28,374 feet. That's more than 5 miles.

Puerto Rico has two towns named Florida. It also has suburbs named Montaña and Cuba.

Puerto Rico has many delicious foods. *Coco frío* is cold coconut milk served in a coconut shell. Beans may be made with a spicy sauce called *sofrito* that is poured over rice. Puerto Rico's national soup, *asopao,* is often made with rice and chicken or seafood. *Lechón asado* (roast pig) is a special holiday dish. Fritters are the island's main "finger food." They are often made out of plantains, a kind of banana. *Flan,* a caramel custard, is a favorite dessert.

Many Puerto Rican towns and rivers kept their Taíno names. Many English words came from Taíno words. For example, *hurricane* came from *juracán* and *canoe* came from *canoa.*

The island has about two holidays a month when shops and offices close. March 22 is Emancipation Day. Puerto Ricans celebrate the day in 1873 when the law ending slavery took effect. Discovery Day is November 19. On this day in 1493, Christopher Columbus arrived in Puerto Rico.

The flavorings for Coca-Cola and Pepsi are made in the town of Cidra. From there they are shipped to bottling plants around the world.

29 USA

1493-1993 500th Anniversary • Columbus Landing in Puerto Rico

On November 19, 1993, the United States issued a Christopher Columbus stamp. It honored the 500th anniversary of Columbus's landing on Puerto Rico.

PUERTO RICO INFORMATION

State flag

Ceiba tree

Area: 3,515 square miles

North-South Distance of Main Island: 39 miles

East-West Distance of Main Island: 111 miles

Coastline: 311 miles

Highest Point: Cerro de Punta, 4,389 feet above sea level

Lowest Point: Sea level, along the coast

Hottest Recorded Temperature: 103° F. (at San Lorenzo, on August 22, 1906)

Coldest Recorded Temperature: 40° F. (at Aibonito, on March 9, 1911)

Full Name: *Estado Libre Asociado de Puerto Rico* (Commonwealth of Puerto Rico)

Origin of Name: *Puerto Rico* means "rich port" in Spanish

Capital: San Juan

Became U.S. Commonwealth: July 25, 1952

Resident Commissioner in U.S. Congress: 1

Commonwealth Senators: 27

Commonwealth Representatives: 51

Municipalities: 78

Song: "La Borinqueña," by Felix Astol y Artés (music) and Manuel Fernández Juncos (words)

Motto: *Joannes est nomen ejus* (Latin for "John is my name," which refers to St. John the Baptist)

Nickname: "Island of Enchantment"

Flag: Adopted in 1952

Flower: Maga

Bird: Reinita

Tree: Ceiba

Animal: Coquí

Some Smaller Islands: Vieques, Culebra, Mona

Some Rivers: La Plata, Loíza, Arecibo, Bayamón

Some Lakes: Cidra, Guajataca, Caonillas

Wildlife: Coquís, paso fino horses, mongooses, Puerto Rican boas, iguanas and other lizards, araña bobas, giant centipedes, bats, reinitas, Puerto Rican parrots, orioles, hummingbirds, owls, doves, gulls, pelicans, boobies, whales, manatees, sea turtles, jellyfish, starfish, seahorses, sea cucumbers, various tropical fish, sharks, herring, lobsters, oysters

Farm Products: Sugar cane, coffee, pineapples, bananas, plantains, coconuts, oranges, beef cattle, milk, chickens, eggs

Manufactured Products: Medicines, electrical machinery, computers, metal products, sugar and other foods, rum, clothing, medical and scientific instruments, plastics, leather products

Fishing Products: Lobsters, clams, oysters, mackerel, tuna, snapper

Mining Products: Sand and gravel, marble, lime, clay, salt

Population: 3,522,037 (1990 Census)

Major Municipalities (1990 Census):

San Juan	437,745	Mayagüez	100,371
Bayamón	220,262	Arecibo	93,385
Ponce	187,749	Guaynabo	92,886
Carolina	177,806	Toa Baja	89,454
Caguas	133,447	Trujillo Alto	61,120

Maga

Left: Reinita
Right: Coquí

Puerto Rico History

Christopher Columbus watching for land

About 2000 B.C.—Archaic Indians, perhaps from the Florida region, reach Puerto Rico

About A.D. 120—Arawak Indians from South America come to Puerto Rico

1400s—Puerto Rico's Indians are calling themselves Taínos; they call Puerto Rico *Borinquén*

1493—Italian explorer Christopher Columbus, sailing for the king and queen of Spain, reaches Puerto Rico

1508—Juan Ponce de León founds Caparra, Puerto Rico's first European settlement, for Spain

1511—The Taínos rebel against the Spaniards but are defeated

1521—Spaniards begin present-day San Juan

1531—A census counts about 500 Spaniards and about 2,000 African slaves in Puerto Rico

1532—Work begins on the fortress known as La Fortaleza

1539—Work begins on the El Morro fortress

1595—English attacks led by Sir Francis Drake fail

1598—The English seize San Juan but are driven out

1625—The Dutch burn San Juan but are driven out

Late 1600s—Ponce is begun

1760—Mayagüez is founded

1793—Humacao is founded

1797—The last English attack, led by Ralph Abercromby, fails

1800—Puerto Rico has thirty-nine towns and over 150,000 people

1868—A revolt organized by Ramón Emeterio Betances is squashed

1873—Slavery is outlawed in Puerto Rico on March 22

1897—Spain agrees to give Puerto Rico some self-government

1898—The United States wins the Spanish-American War against Spain and takes control of Puerto Rico

1903—The University of Puerto Rico is founded

1917—In March, President Woodrow Wilson signs the Jones Act, making the people of Puerto Rico United States citizens

1917-18—Puerto Rico sends 18,000 soldiers to help the United States win World War I

1929-39—During the Great Depression, Puerto Ricans suffer from extreme poverty and disease

1932—Puerto Rico's women win the right to vote

1937—In the "Ponce Massacre," 21 people die and more than 100 are wounded during a political march in Ponce

1941-45—About 65,000 people from Puerto Rico help the United States win World War II

1946—Jesús T. Piñero is named the first native Puerto Rican governor under United States rule

1948—Luis Muñoz Marín becomes the first governor to be elected by the people of Puerto Rico

1950—Puerto Rico's population is 2.2 million

1952—On July 25, Puerto Rico becomes a United States commonwealth

1967—Puerto Ricans vote to continue as a commonwealth

1977—Widespread drought hurts farming in Puerto Rico

1985—About 200 people die in floods caused by a three-day rainstorm

1989—Hurricane Hugo slams into Puerto Rico

1990—Puerto Rico's population tops 3.5 million

1993—In a close vote, Puerto Ricans choose to remain a commonwealth rather than become a state or an independent country

American medical officers at Coamo Springs after the Spanish-American War in 1898

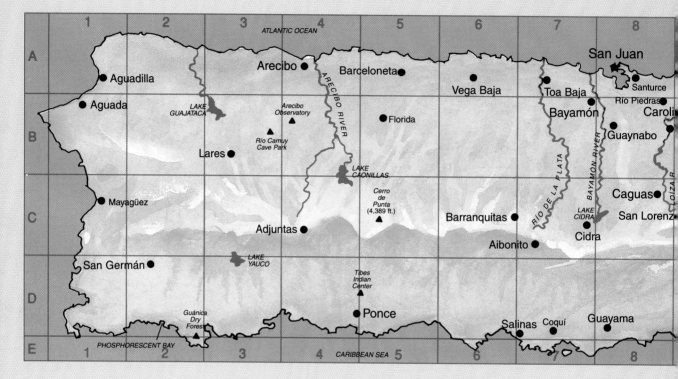

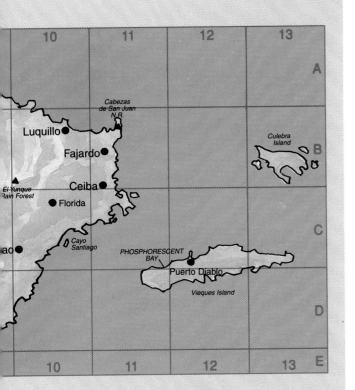

GLOSSARY

archaic: Very old

cactus: A plant known for its ability to live in dry places

capital: A city that is the seat of government

capitol: The building in which the government meets

climate: The typical weather of a region

commonwealth: A place that has self-government but that has close ties with a larger country

coral reef: An ocean ridge created by tiny animals called corals

emancipation: The act of freeing people

extraterrestrial: From beyond the planet earth

Hispanic: A person of Spanish-speaking background

hurricane: A huge storm that forms over an ocean

independence: Freedom to run one's country's government

island: A piece of land surrounded by water

61

million: A thousand thousand (1,000,000)

municipality: A Puerto Rican governmental unit similar to a county in the United States

observatory: A place where scientists study the heavens or other aspects of nature

paso fino: A small horse bred over the centuries in Puerto Rico that is known for its delicate way of walking

phosphorescent: Glowing

plantation: A very large farm

plaza: A public square

population: The number of people in a place

revolutionary: Relating to overthrowing a government

trade wind: A tropical ocean wind that blows all the time

tropical: Relating to the warm regions north and south of the Equator

volcano: An opening through which materials erupt from inside the earth; also, the mountains built from the eruptions

INDEX

Page numbers in boldface type indicate illustrations.

ABOUT THE AUTHORS

Dennis and Judith Fradin have coauthored several books in the From Sea to Shining Sea series. The Fradins both graduated from Northwestern University in 1967. Dennis has been a professional writer for twenty years, and has published 150 books. His works for Childrens Press include the Young People's Stories of Our States series, the Disaster! series, and the Thirteen Colonies series. Judith earned her M.A. in literature from Northwestern University and taught high-school and college English for many years. The Fradins, who are the parents of Anthony, Diana, and Michael, live in Evanston, Illinois.